Andrea Holst
Daniela Bolze

FIRST AID

How to save your horse in an emergency

CADMOS
EQUESTRIAN

Contents

The healthy horse 3

The sick horse 5

   Possible visible symptoms 5

The daily check-up 7
   Overall impression 7
   Feeding habits 7
   Movement 7
   Condition 8
   Controlling the environment 8

These should be included in every first aid kit 9

Coping with an emergency .. 10

Illnesses 12
   Wounds 12
      Foreign bodies 12
      Fresh wounds 13
      Bandaging wounds 13
      Bleeding wounds 17
      Pressure bandage 18
      Old wounds 19
      Puncture wounds 19
      Prevention 19
   Bruising/pulled muscles 20
   Colic 21
   Cast horse 23
   Choking 24
   Hoof injuries 25
   Laminitis 26

   Nutrition-induced laminitis 26
   Acute laminitis 27
   Toxic laminitis 27
   Drug-related laminitis 27
   Azoturia 28
   Eye injuries 29
   Fractures 30
   Shock 31

First aid out hacking 32

The publisher advises that all of the treatments described in this book should only be undertaken in consulation with a veterinary surgeon, and can accept no liability for their results.

Imprint

Copyright of orginal edition © 2003 by
Cadmos Verlag GmbH, Brunsbek
Copyright of this edition © 2004 Cadmos Verlag
Translated by Desiree Gerber
Project Management: Editmaster Co. Ltd.
Design and typesetting: Ravenstein, Verden
Photographs: Daniela Bolze, Dr. Andrea Holst
Printed by Grindeldruck, Hamburg

All rights reserved
Copying or storage in electronic media is permited only with the prior permissio n of the publisher
Printed in Germany.

ISBN 3-86127-940-1

A shiny coat, well-developed muscles and not too much fat over the ribs are all good signs of a healthy horse.

The healthy horse

As with people, normally one can see immediately whether or not a horse is healthy. A healthy horse will participate with its natural environment, in keeping with its temperament. It will prick its ears in the direction of any noise. It will turn its head in the direction and look with clear and alert eyes. It will approach the stable door or the paddock fence with curiosity when a person stands there. The nostrils are dry and without any discharge. Its coat is shiny and smooth, without being caked – although this is different in winter. The condition of the coat should reflect the season, breed and way the horse is kept. Robust breeds and horses that live out all year round will naturally have a thicker, more tousled coat than the thoroughbred-types or warmbloods that are stabled. The skin and coat are the horse's first line of protection against the elements.

A healthy horse has a healthy appetite and should swiftly finish his feed. Apart from the compound feeds (cubes, mixes) a horse needs forage (hay, grass, straw), according to his job and its energy requirements, and this must be available daily for a healthy digestive system.

First Aid

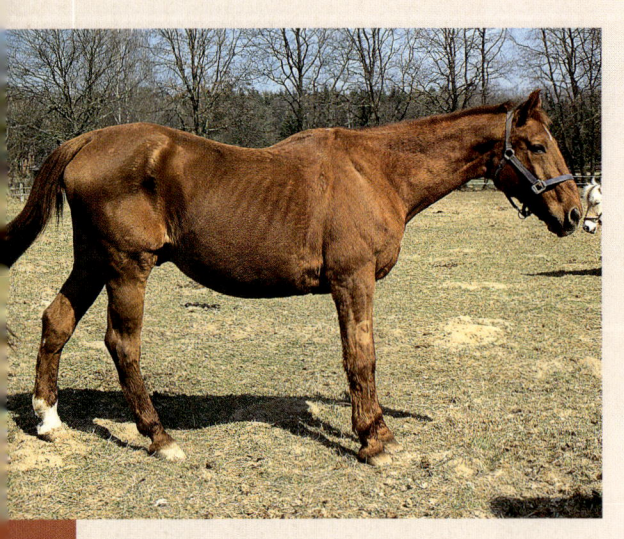

When horses lose weight for no apparent reason, the vet must be called.

After the meal there should be no leftovers and no signs of quidding (food being spilt from the mouth as the horse eats), which could be an indication of teeth problems.

The horse's physique will depend on its breed. This, however, does not mean that visible ribs and hipbones or layers of fat are acceptable. The ribs should be felt with a light touch, but should not be visible.

The droppings should be hard round balls that are brown or dark green, depending on the feed the horse gets. The horse should pass droppings daily without any problems. The same should be the case for urination and this should be a light yellow colour.

The horse must put even weight on all four legs and walk without any sign of lameness. There should be no swollen areas on the body or the legs and especially no warm areas. Depending on the age, breed and character of the horse, it should have a natural tendency for movement – in the paddock as well as in the company of people.

The horse should be wormed every six to twelve weeks. The growth of the hooves, regardless of whether they are shod or not, must be controlled by a professional farrier every six to ten weeks.

> Normal values:
> **Pulse** between 28 and 42 beats per minute
> **Body temperature** 37 to 38 degrees Celsius (100 to 101 degrees Fahrenheit).
> **Respiratory rate** at rest between 8 and 16 breaths per minute

The more we separate horses from their natural habitat (which is the same for ponies and warmbloods) the more we have to ensure we provide alternative means that keep the horse functioning in a healthy way: be it feeding (with many small meals per day), demands for movement (sufficiently controlled), the particular aptitude of the breed, taking the age of the horse into consideration, or social contact (horses are herd animals that require social contact for their physical well-being) in fresh air.

It is the responsibility of the horse owner to be well-informed and knowledgeable in order to keep the animal in an environment that is beneficial for the psychological as well as the physiological needs of the horse.

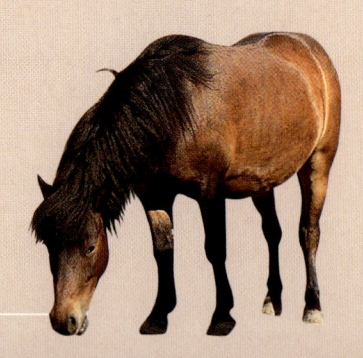

A dirty tail and legs are often signs of a disturbance in the digestive system.

The sick horse

A sick horse can be recognised by the absence of all or any of the signs of good health. The owner will often notice immediately that something is amiss with a sick horse. The better the owner knows his horse, the finer the nuances that something is wrong and the sooner the correct response can be put into action.

Possible visible symptoms

Horses can seem completely downcast. One will often see the head hanging, little or no reaction to outside stimulation, they might look listless and weak and have no appetite. The eyes can be clouded and in some cases even inflamed and weepy. Some horses get deep hollows above the eyes. They will eventually cough – no matter whether after feeding, at rest or in movement. This will often be accompanied by a nasal discharge. The gums will be pale and the horse will show the flehmen response more than is normal. Some horses will press their lips together as a response to the pain, and even grind their teeth together. The coat is dull, and old wounds stand out. The horse does not want to move, and when it does, it walks with extreme difficulty on stiff legs and drags the

First Aid

Horses can also look downcast. There is something wrong with this horse.

feet or seems lame. An ill horse may stand with an abnormal posture or a particularly rounded back.

The horse will swish its tail more (without the annoyance of insects), move restlessly, kick its abdomen, and shows more itchiness than normal. The horse will lie down more often and roll. It will even lie down flat at unusual times (for example when it would normally be time to eat or play). The horse will often look at its abdomen, show signs of restlessness, and might paw the ground for no apparent reason. The horse will breathe with difficulty or more rapidly than normal (more than 16 breaths per minute). It might sweat spontaneously and has fever (more than 38.5 degrees celcius/102 degrees Fahrenheit).

The droppings can be too hard and dry, or too soft, even a watery diarrhoea. If there are no droppings at all, the situation is serious. The urine will have a strong smell and be discoloured.

The daily check-up

Exterior wounds or bruises are easy to notice and the owner should check for these every day as a matter of course. Every horse owner should be able to perform a daily check-up on his horse. In reality, however, the average owner has to juggle a job with visits two or three times a week to the stable. In this case it is important that the owner finds a stand-in person who can perform checks on a daily base. But the owner must at the very least make enough time to perform this task at least once a week himself.

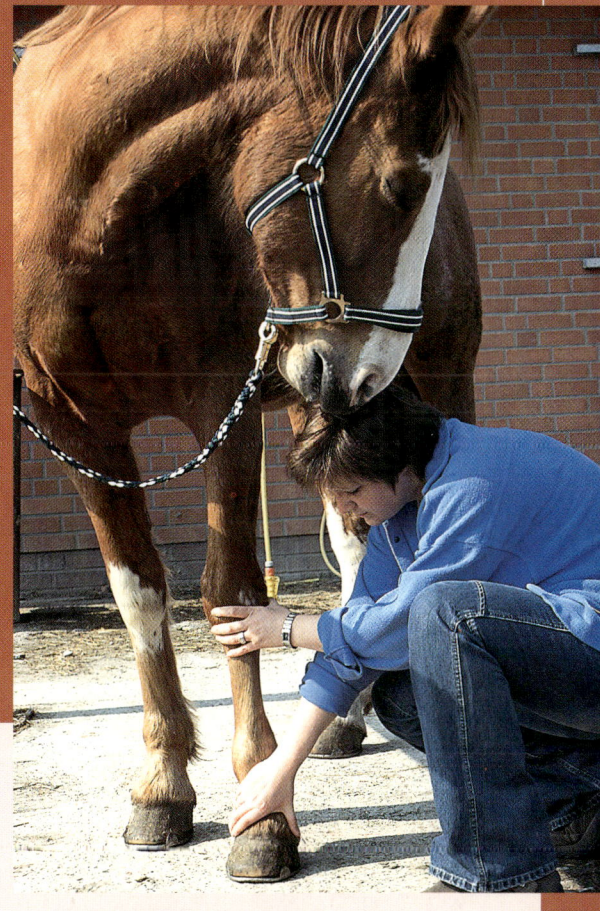

The owner should frequently check the horse for wounds, cuts and bruises

Overall impression

Take time to observe your horse whilst it is feeding and moving around. Does he move differently, has he a different mood than normal – tired, frantic, hyperactive, lethargic? Does the horse show any of the signs mentioned under "The sick horse"? Does the horse react irritably with a tail swish, or snap when touched or when the girth is tightened?

Feeding habits

Does the horse eat with an even grinding movement, or does he leave balls of food behind? Do you see any food that stays wedged in his cheeks, or does he make unusual noises when eating? Does the horse finish all his food? Does the horse have a foul smell coming from his mouth? Does he drink more or less than would be considered normal?

Are there any droppings, and what is their state?

Movement

Does the horse move without any sign of lameness and according to the rhythm in both the walk and trot on a hard surface? Is the horse supple and normal under saddle?

Is the horse reluctant to move into another gait, does he resist, feel tight or have an inferior bend to one side (more than would be considered normal for the horse)?

Inspect the hooves every day for foreign objects or cracks. Are the shoes still tight, or could playing in the paddock loosen them?

Condition

When brushing the horse, try and stroke it with the naked hand all over its body. This is the only way to become aware of small scratches, swollen areas, hot spots, changes in the skin or coat and painful regions. Take exceptional care on the legs and the fetlocks of the horse. Remember to check the anus, as well as the teats in mares and the sheath in geldings and stallions.

Controlling the environment

The second most important factor in maintaining a horse's health – after a near-natural environment with superior feeding – is a safe environment, for horses are naturally inquisitive and are often swift and violent in their movement. The stable should be checked frequently for sharp objects such as nails, pointed edges and stones and broken glass. The stabled horse must be free from such dangers in his box; there must not even be a slight chance that a horse can hurt itself on such dangerous objects. The horse should also be kept without a head collar in the stable.

Ask yourself the question: are there any defects in the walls which the horse can snag against, or does the floor have any gaps that the horse can be trapped in?

Is the fence of the paddock safe, or can you find nails protruding or broken poles where the horse might hurt itself? What about barbed wire fencing, which one can definitely do without in the vicinity of horses? Are all the electric fence straps tight, or do they flap in the wind? Are there any sharp instruments or tools lying around which the horses might step onto? Are there any sharp stones, burrows or cement blocks, on or in which a horse can get a hoof trapped?

Is the feed bin clean, installed in such a way that the horse will not get his head or his hoof caught and is able to eat in peace (even when the horse is low in the pecking order)?

All areas where the horse may be turned out must be free of any poisonous plants.

A thorough inspection of the environment will reduce the likelihood of injury from the onset.

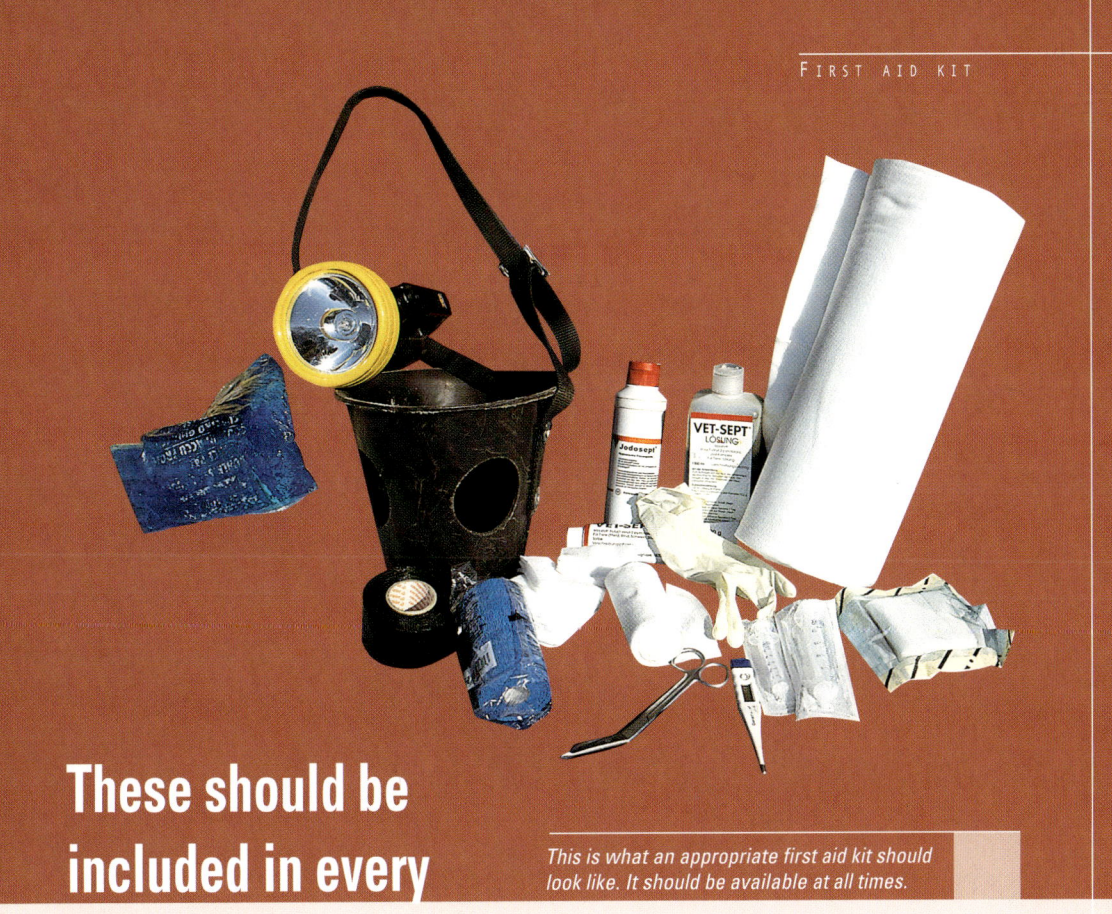

FIRST AID KIT

These should be included in every first aid kit

This is what an appropriate first aid kit should look like. It should be available at all times.

Truthfully, is your first aid kit a dusty box full of mouldy bandages and a few wound ointments that have passed their sell-by date? The investment in a properly closing, waterproof container or a cupboard with comprehensive contents is worth the effort and can save lives. Your vet will without doubt be happy to advise in the compilation of a first aid kit.

The following should be included:
Antiseptic solution
Mild disinfectant
Bandage material:
- Crepe bandages
- Self-adhesive bandages
- Cotton wool
- Gauze
- Antibiotic tulle
- Clean towels
- Cold bandages are not a must but can be helpful

Single use latex gloves
Digital thermometer
Torch
Muzzle
Scissors
A list with the most important telephone numbers:
- The horse's vet
- The vet clinic with directions
- Farrier
- Emergency number for the rider
- Owner's telephone number
- Horse transport

First Aid

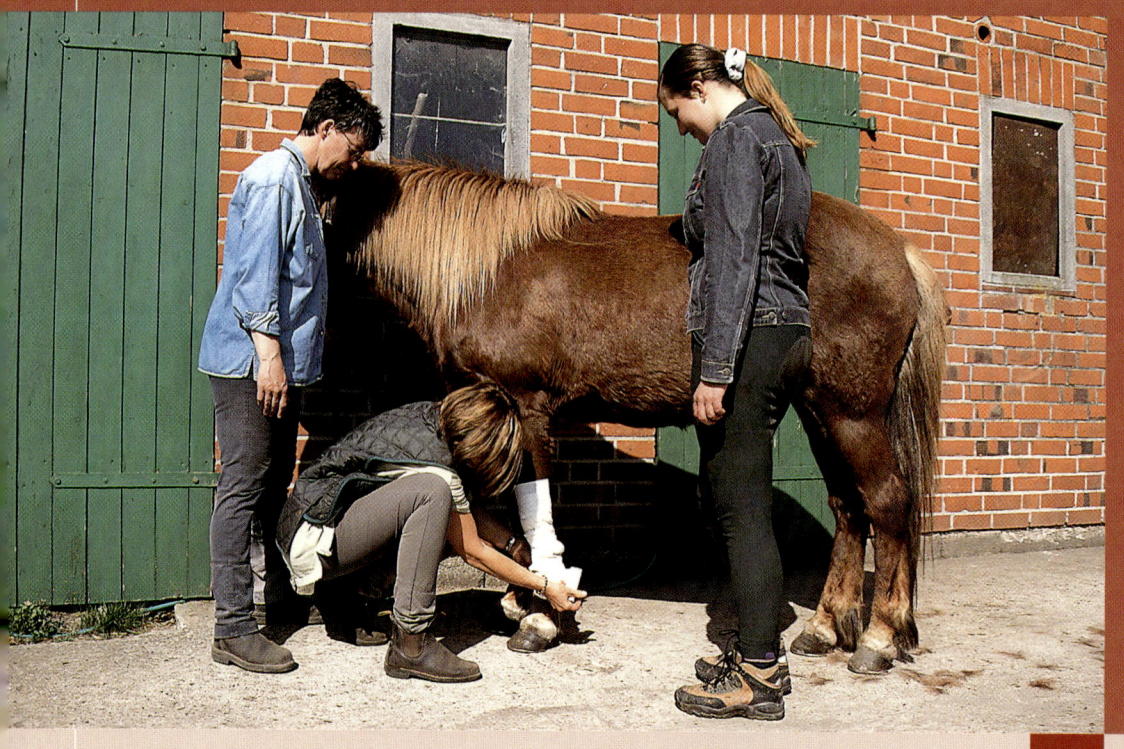

It is a good idea to practise putting on a bandage; this will ensure that there is less stress in an emergency.

Coping with an emergency

By its very nature, an emergency comes as a completely unexpected event. You can, however, do something to be prepared for such a situation:
1. Keep the first aid kit up to date at all times.
2. Practise techniques to calm a horse down, and bandaging techniques; this will cause less stress in an emergency.
3. Win your horse's confidence so that it will follow you even in emergency situations.

An emergency is a situation of stress for both horse and rider. This makes it even more important to stay calm:
- Get a complete grasp of the situation.
- What exactly is the nature of the emergency?
- How serious is the injury/symptom?
- Is the horse in a safe position?
- Are other horses or people injured or in danger?

COPING WITH AN EMERGENCY

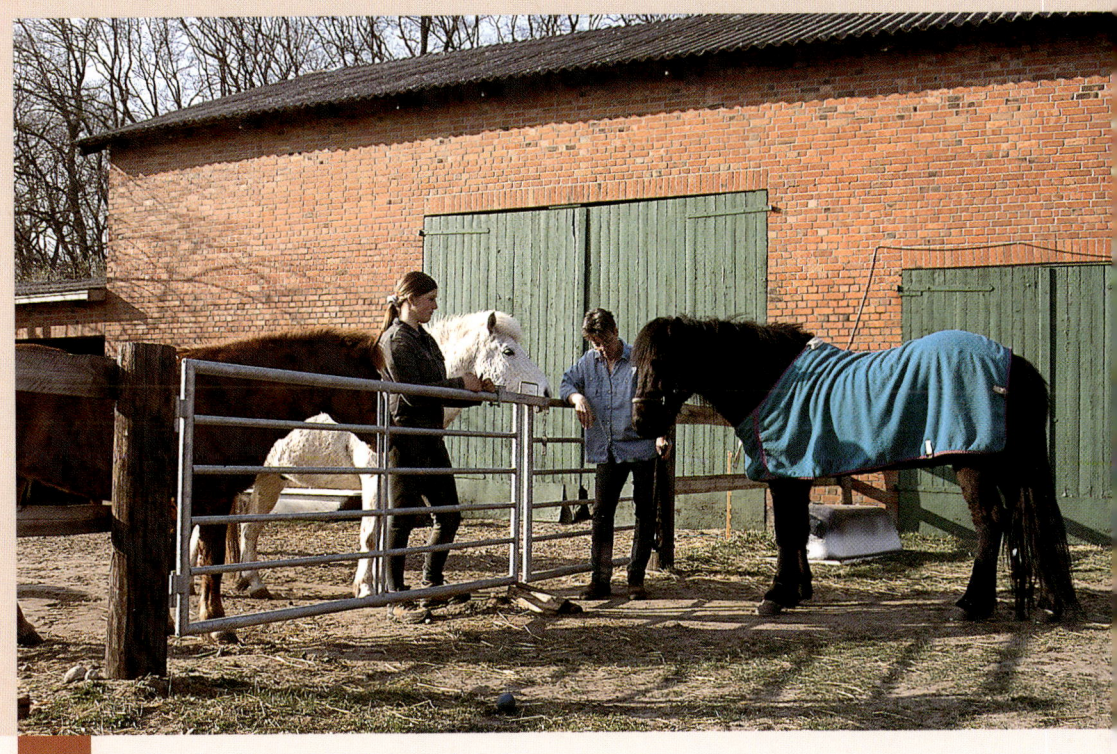

The injured or ill horse should be kept calm in the company of friends while waiting for the vet.

- Make sure that there are responsible people available to hold your horse or see to other matters.
- Call the vet and give a detailed account of the injury/symptoms.
- Provide light and clean water. If at all possible, running water is better.
- Place the horse in a stress-free location and keep him calm and safe. If you are not able to do that, fetch a helper who can take over this job. Other animals should be kept away from the injured horse, but not out of sight completely.
- Give the horse the appropriate kind of attention described in this book. Provide first aid for the horse.
- When necessary, arrange transport to the vet clinic, if the circumstances should require.

First Aid

Illnesses

It is possible that one or more injuries can give rise to the same symptoms. First aid deals with the situation until the vet arrives. The owner cannot replace the visit from the vet!

Wounds

1. Main causes:

It is possible that one or more injuries can give rise to the same symptoms. First aid deals with the situation until the vet arrives. The owner cannot replace the visit from the vet!

2. Symptoms:
- Open wounds
- Blood
- Swelling around the wound within a couple of hours
- Lameness.

3. First aid:
This applies for all injuries with wounds: the horse must be kept calm and care must be taken to stop the wound becoming soiled until the vet arrives.

Foreign bodies
- Big foreign bodies should be left in the wound, as they might have penetrated a blood vessel. Removing the foreign body could cause excessive blood loss under these circumstances.

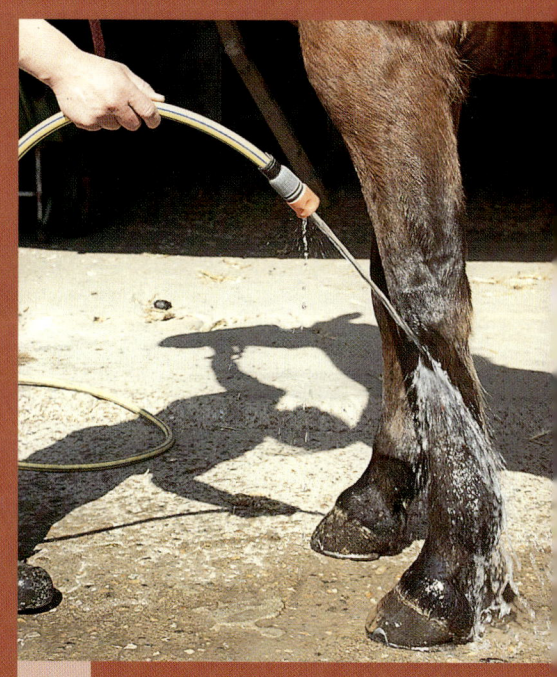

Wounds can be cleaned with clean running water...

...or by syringing with an antiseptic solution.

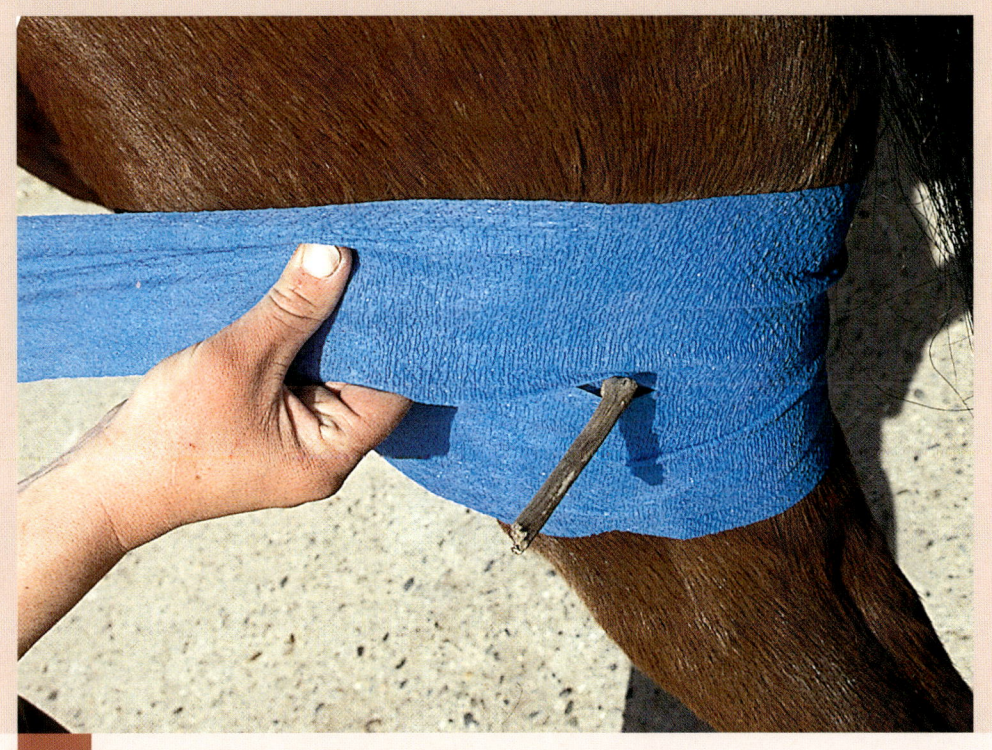

Big foreign bodies should be left in the wound and secured in place until the vet arrives. Removal can cause blood vessels to rupture.

- The foreign body should be secured in place to cause as little movement as possible, and the vet must be summoned immediately.

Fresh wounds
- The wound must be cleaned with clean, running water, on and around the wound. Nothing should be added to the water and the area should not be dried with a towel or anything else.
- The area around the wound should then be treated with an antiseptic solution (using a syringe, but without actually going on the wound itself).
- A sterile bandage should be used to cover the wound. (Take care, the horse might object to this.)

Bandaging wounds
a) Cannon bone bandage
Cover the area with sterile gauze. Wrap cotton wool around the whole length of the cannon bone and include the fetlock joint. Make sure that the cotton wool is not creased. Start in the middle of the cannon and roll a crepe bandage around the leg with moderate tension and without any knots or creases, moving in the direction of the fetlock joint. From the fetlock the direction must reverse to the top of the cannon bone, to below the

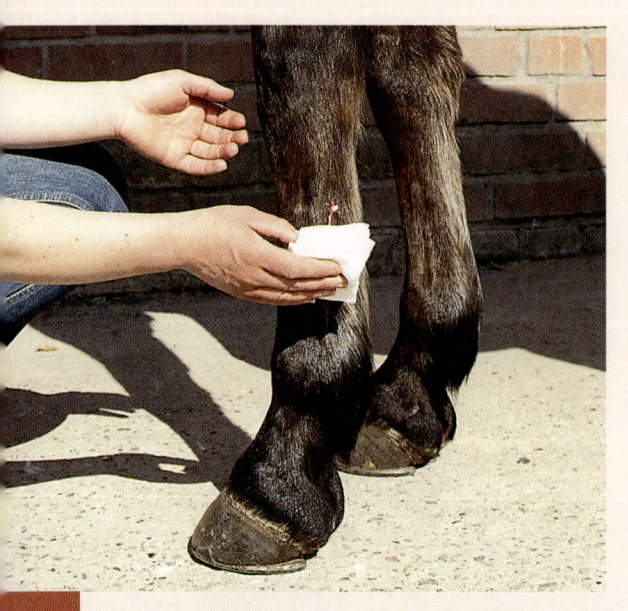

First Aid

The cleaned wound is covered with sterile gauze …

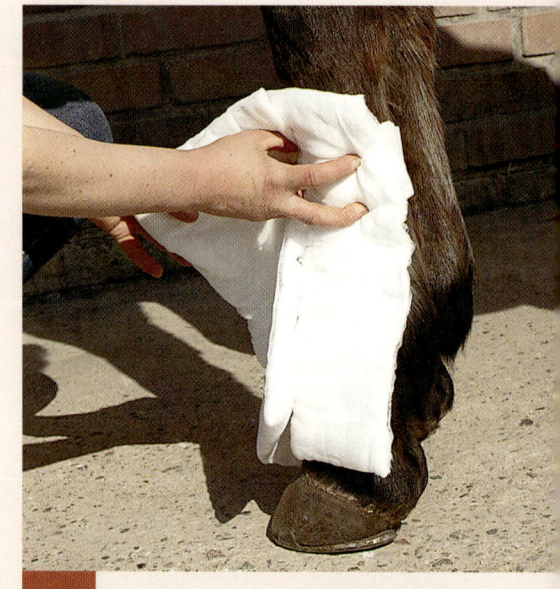

… thick cotton wool is wrapped around the leg…

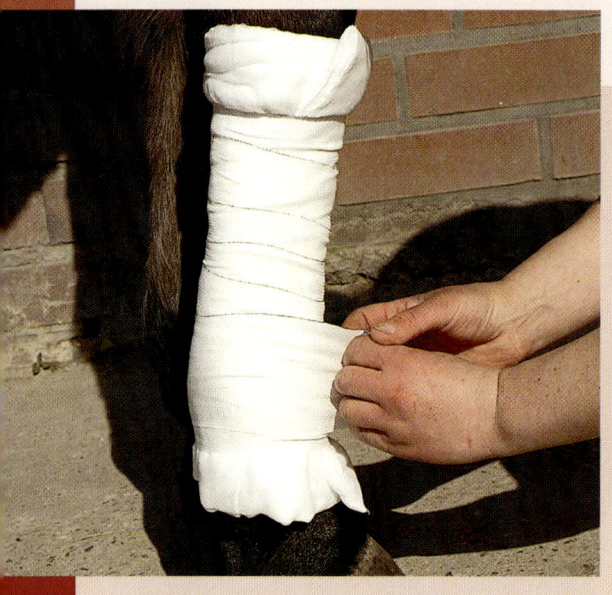

… an elastic bandage is then wrapped around the leg …

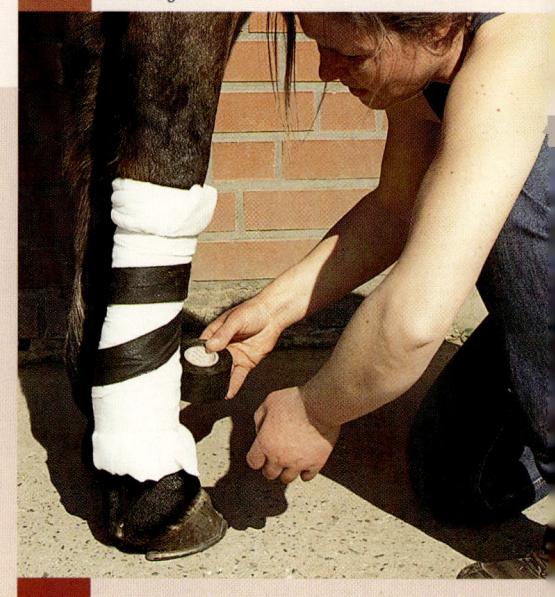

… and fastened with tape – without tying a knot.

knee/hock and return to the fetlock once more. The layers of bandage should be no more than three. The cotton wool must always be obviously detectable for about two centimetres at the top and bottom of the bandage.

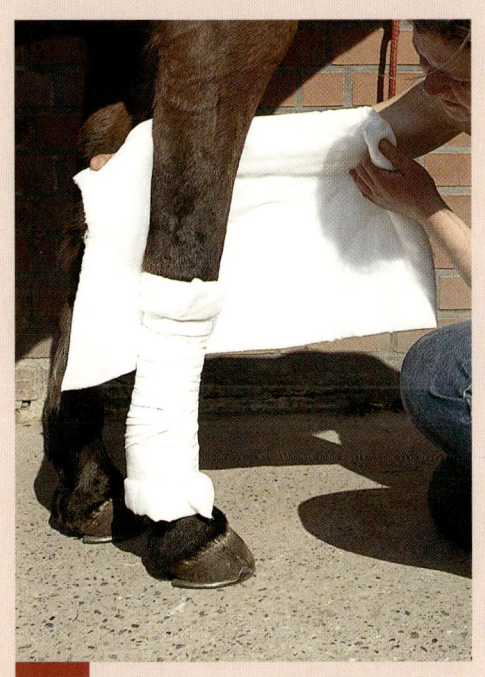

ILLNESSES

Wrap the cotton wool over and above the bandage on the lower leg …

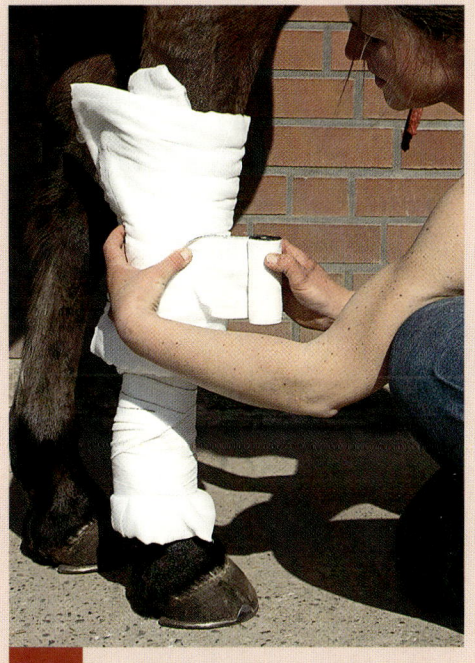

… roll the elastic bandage from the middle …

… and wrap the lower bandage with the upper bandage.

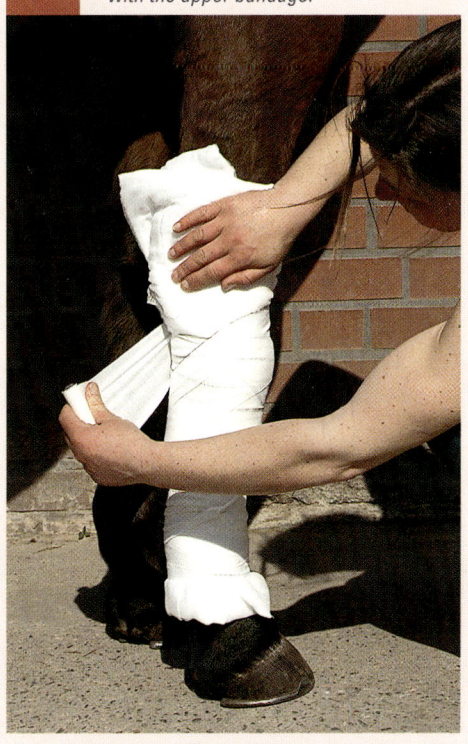

b) High bandage

This is a bandage above the knee in the front leg and above the stifle in the hind leg. Start the bandage as described previously. Cover the wound with sterile gauze and pad with cotton wool, starting at least 10 cm over the lower leg bandage and moving to above the wound if possible. Wrap the elastic bandage around the leg, starting in the middle and moving down one third of the lower leg and returning to the upper leg without any creases in the bandage. At least two centimetres of cotton wool must remain above the end of the bandage at the top.

The higher up a leg a bandage has to go, the more difficult it is to secure. At this stage it is only important for the bandage to stay in position until the vet arrives.

First Aid

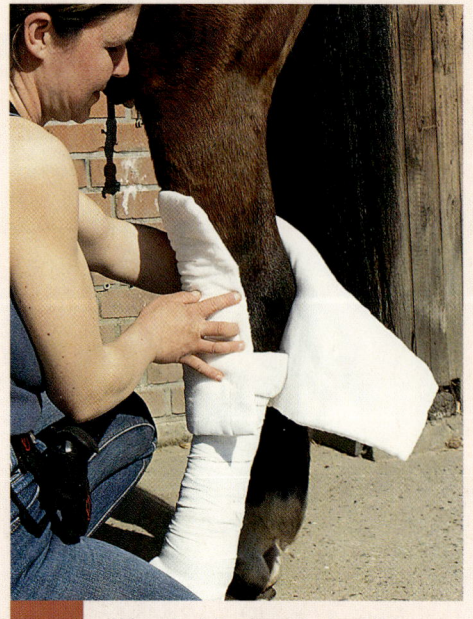

When the injury is on the hock, it is better to first wrap a bandage around the cannon bone.

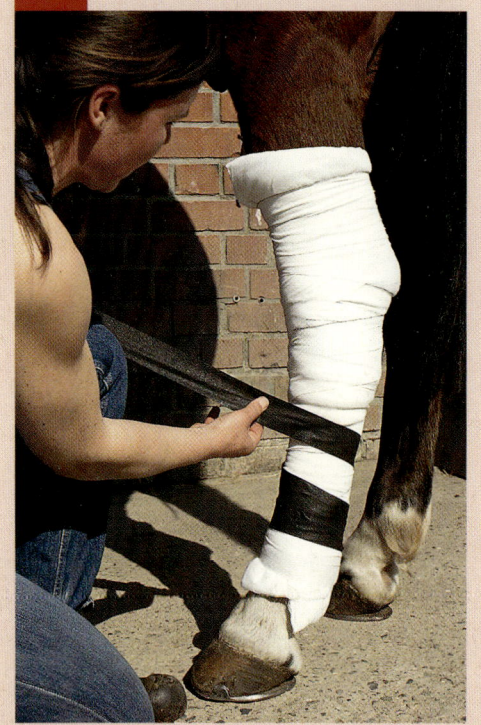

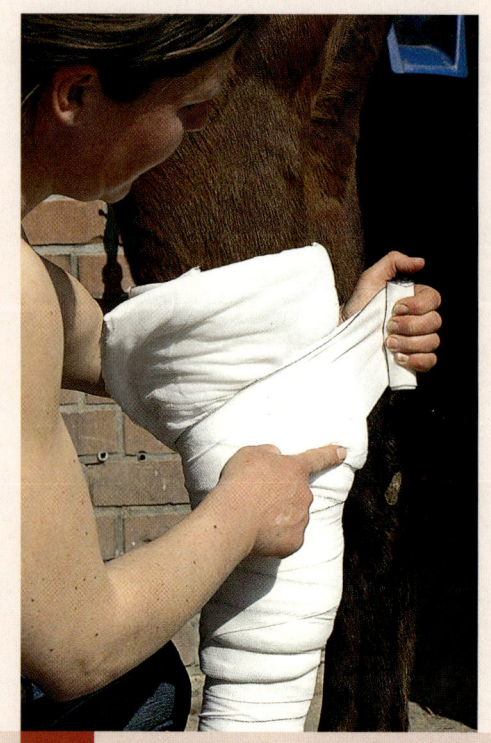

Tie both bandages with tape, without constricting.

Pad the wound with lots of cotton wool and leave some freedom for movement around the joint when the elastic bandage is wrapped around.

When the injury is on the knee itself, it might be better to do without a bandage when both the rider and horse are panicky.

A bandage around the lower leg before the upper bandage might seem to involve more effort, but in the end it is worth the exertion. In the first instance it will prevent the upper bandage from slipping, and secondly it will prevent the cannon bone from swelling to a large extent.

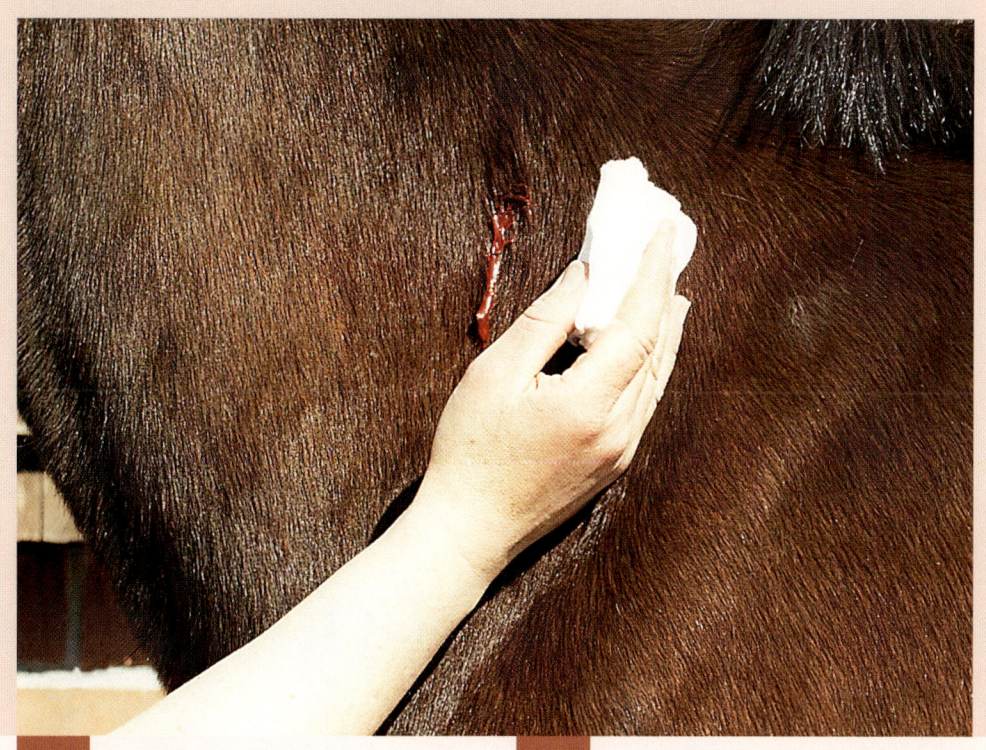

Strong-bleeding wounds on the neck cannot be bandaged. Cover the wound with sterile gauze …

… and press a clean towel or something similar on the wound until the vet arrives.

Bleeding wounds

Heavy bleeding
In this case a blood vessel has been injured:
- Clean with pure running water.
- Cover with sterile gauze.
- Wrap a pressure bandage around when it is a leg injury.
- When the injury is elsewhere, press a clean towel (cover with sterile gauze first!) on the wound until the vet arrives.

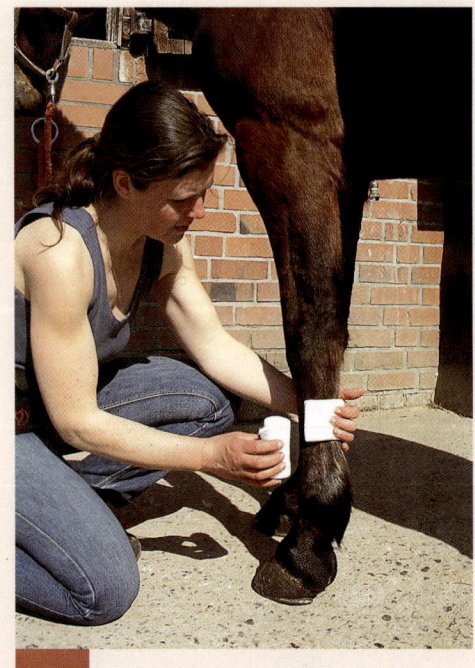

First Aid

Pressure bandage

A pressure bandage will stop the flow of blood. The basic application is the same as with the cannon bone bandage. To make it into a pressure bandage you need to press about 20 folded tissues or a clean, rolled elastic bandage on the sterile gauze before the cotton wool and bandage is wrapped around the leg. When the blood soaks through the bandage, do not remove it, but add another layer of bandage until the vet arrives.

A pressure bandage is easy to apply on a leg. Cover the wound with sterile gauze …

… press the rolled bandage/folded tissues on top …

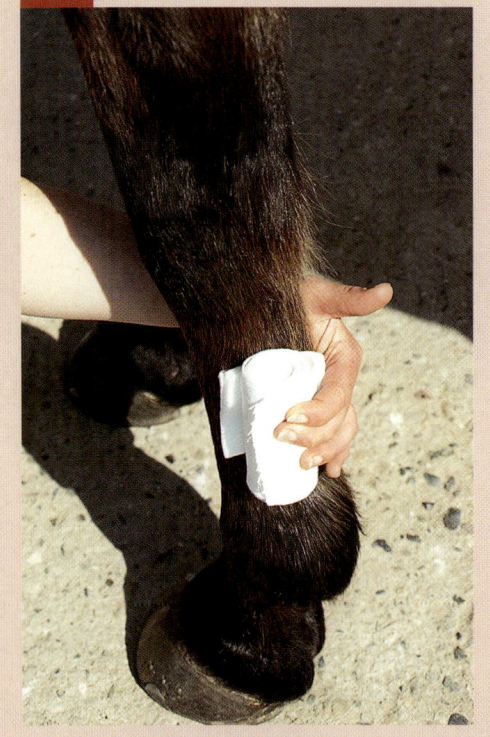

…wrap cotton wool around and then the elastic bandage.

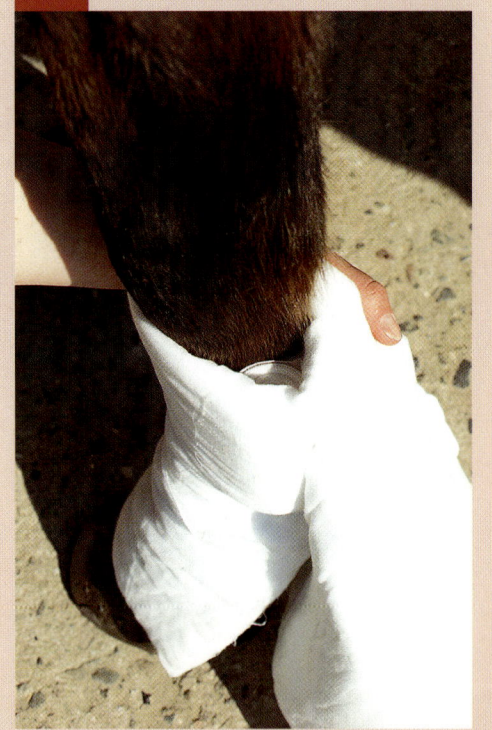

Illnesses

Old wounds
- Clean with luke-warm water.
- Soften the scab with wet gauze, dipped in water containing disinfectant.
- Clean with antiseptic.

Puncture wounds
A puncture wound, skin irritation or something similar can cause an acute inflammation of the tissues and lymphatic circulation. In the horse this situation can rapidly lead to swelling of one or more limbs.

- Identify the wound.
- Clean thoroughly as for old wounds.
- Apply ice or cold pack.

Wet towels and cold packs are great to cool a wound, but are difficult to keep in place and can seldom be applied for more that a few minutes at a time (this is only convenient when the horse is quiet).

Prevention
Wounds cannot be prevented altogether in the life of horses. However, careful monitoring of the environment will help prevent the risk of major accidents and careless injuries.

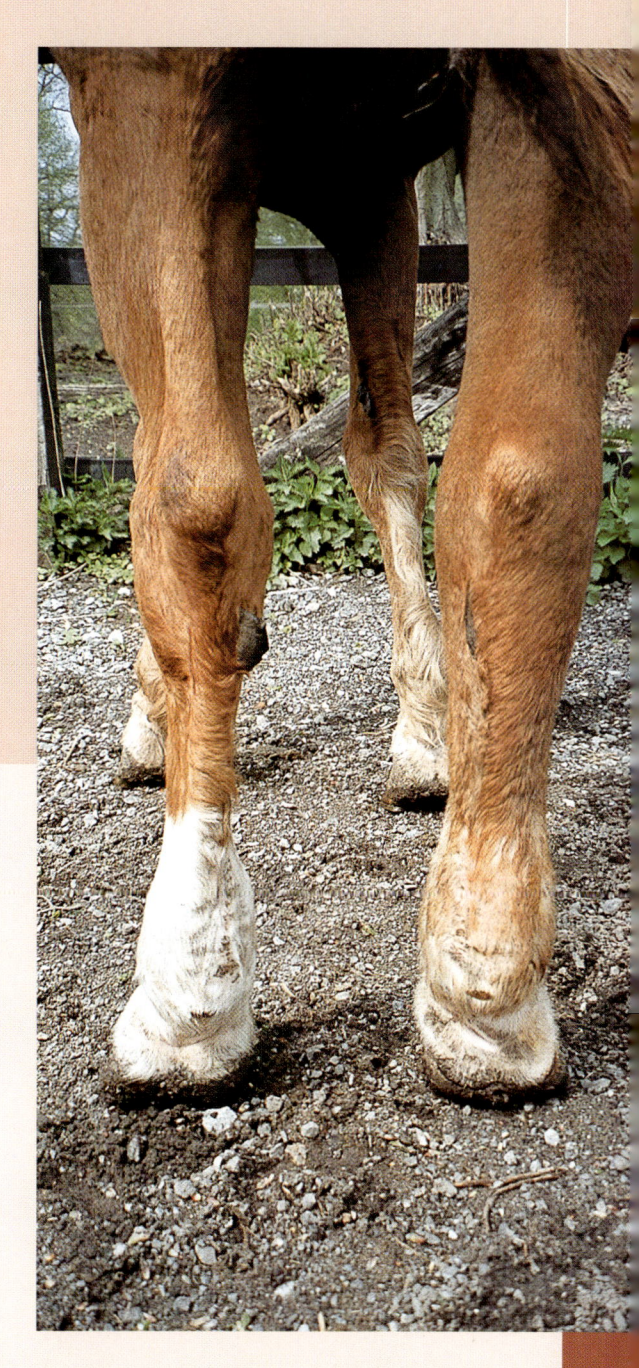

Puncture wounds can cause swelling in the legs.

First Aid

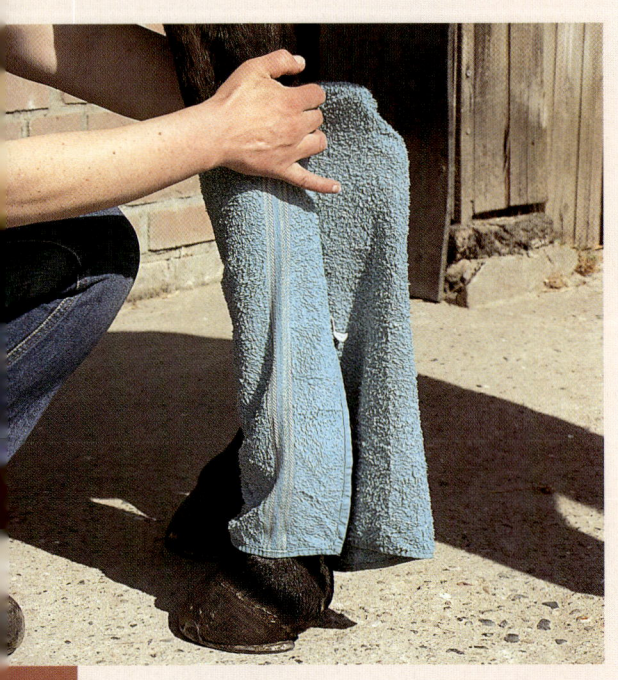

Wrap a wet towel around the horse's leg...

...secure as well as possible with an elastic bandage.

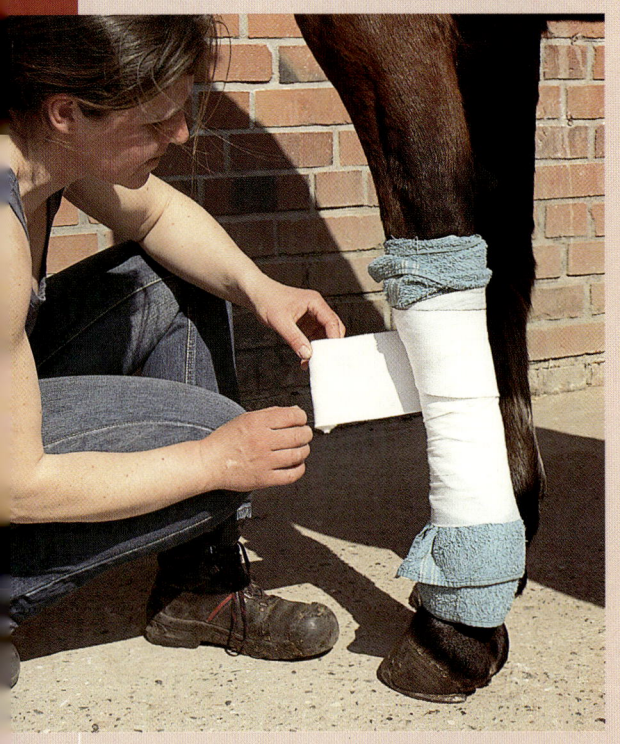

Bruising/pulled muscles

1. Main causes:
Incoherent steps, sudden extra demands and stretching, a demanding rider, bad going, spooking and a panicking horse can all be causes for bruising or pulled muscles.

2. Symptoms:
- Lameness.
- Difficulty in movement (the horse is stiff, does not bend its neck or rump).
- Tail bent and carried to one side.
- Swelling.
- Heat.
- Painful when touched.

3. First aid:
- Calm the horse down.
- Cool the area with cold running water.
- Wrap with cold packs or wet towels.

4. Prevention:
it is very important to warm up the horse properly when riding. Ride in walk for at least 15 minutes until the joints are supple enough to move without any difficulty.

Take care when the going is bad. Do not let frisky horses out on frozen or slippery paddocks. When the horse has poor conformation, everything should be done to correct or help the situation, for example remedial shoeing.

Uneasy rolling and kicking the stomach are sure signs of colic.

Colic

As is the case with all herbivores, the horse can have difficulty breaking down cellulose, and this will have an impact on its sensitive digestive system. The horse will get stomach ache. This can be so acute that it can lead to circulatory failure and even death.

1. **Main causes:**
- Bad food (dirty, mouldy).
- Abrupt change of feed.
- Lack of movement.
- Stress (change of stable, paddock, competition, fights with other horses).
- Change in the weather.
- Lack of water.
- Taking in too much sand.
- Parasites.

2. **Symptoms:**
- The horse does not eat or eats very little.
- Pawing.
- Lying down often, uneasy rolling.
- Tail swishing (without insects).
- Looking at the stomach, kicking the stomach.
- Sweating.
- Loss of interest.
- Loss of movement.
- Pained expression (nostrils pulled up, tight lips, grinding, enlarged pupils).

3. **First aid:**
- Remove the feed immediately.
- Place a sweat rug on the horse, depending on the time of year, to relieve the heart from working too hard.

First Aid

When horses take in too much sand as they search for food, it may lead to colic.

Bad, mouldy food should not appear on the menu for horses.

- Lead the horse calmly at a walk (do not lunge).
- Do not allow the horse to roll (the intestine can become twisted).
- Administer nux vomica c30 globules (a homoeopathic remedy that relieves cramping): dissolve two to three globules in water and syringe directly into the horse's mouth every 30 minutes.

4. **Prevention:**
Always check the feed and the grass in the paddock. Try to avoid the causes listed above under 1.

Loosely put the lunge reins around the fetlocks of the lower leg to ensure they come undone easily when the horse gets up.

Cast horse

It can happen every so often that a horse will become cast in the stable. This usually means that they cannot get up by themselves. This may be because they are too close to the wall or their legs are caught.

Do not just run to the horse's side, fetch an extra person to help (and perhaps a third one to help at the horse's head). Return with two lunge reins. Releasing the horse from a cast position can be dangerous for the people involved, as the horse can suddenly jump up in a panic and tread on them.

If the legs of the horse are caught, they have to be freed before the lunge reins are placed in position. Depending on the circumstances, it may be necessary to remove some beams to free the horse. Take care when doing this not to frighten the horse, and be careful not to get within kicking range of the horse's legs.

Put the lunge reins around the fetlocks of the legs on the ground. Agree with your partner, and pull at the same time, rolling the horse over. Be careful to position yourself with space behind you, and take care to get out of the way fast enough.

In some instances, especially when the horse panics, it is not possible to free the horse. The danger of being hurt is too great. The best action in such a case is to wait calmly until the vet arrives to administer a calming injection.

Examine the horse as soon as it gets up for any injuries.

First Aid

- Coughing.
- Sporadic tension in the lower muscles of the neck.
- Restlessness.
- Sweating.
- Difficulty in breathing.
- Refusal to eat.

3. First aid:
- This is a real emergency: call the vet immediately!
- Calm the horse.
- Cover the horse with a sweat sheet.
- Administer nux vomica globuli c30 (two globules under the lips).

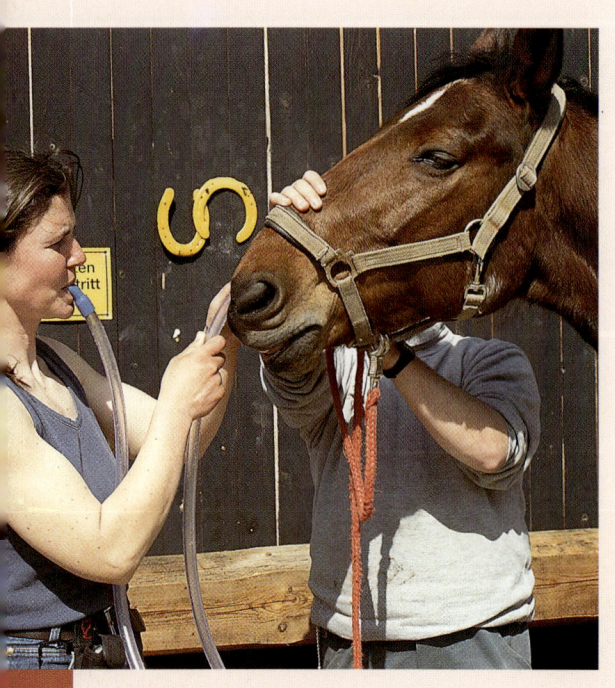

The digestive canals can be squirted with water with the use of a nasal tube.

Choking

1. Main causes:
- Quality of the feed (pellets need lots of saliva and greedy horses do not produce sufficient amounts).
- Vegetable or fruit pieces that are cut too small.
- Teeth problems.
- Stress.
- Jealousy of another horse's food.

2. Symptoms:
- Watery-slimy discharge from the mouth or nostrils. The discharge can also be clear and colourless and gush out in vast amounts.
- Lowered head.

4. Prevention:
Soak food for long enough. Feed only whole carrots, and cut apples into big pieces. Feed composite foods/grain and vegetables/fruit separately. Provide a stress-free environment to feed in. Get a vet to examine the horse's teeth at least once a year.

Vegetables and composite food should be fed separately. Do not cut carrots and apples into small pieces.

Illnesses

Hoof injuries

1. Main causes
- Sharp objects.
- Torn-off horse shoe, taking some of the wall of the hoof with it.

2. Symptoms:
- Lameness (all degrees, from hardly to very lame).
- Warm hoof.
- Pulsating hoof (there are two blood vessels to the left and right behind the fetlock, when inflammation is present a heavy pulse can be felt here).
- Dried blood under the hoof when a cut or puncture wound is present.
- Foreign bodies stuck in the hoof.

3. First aid:
- Remove foreign bodies with appropriate tools.
- Clean with running cold water.
- Clean with antiseptic (use a big syringe for this).
- Calm the horse.
- Wrap a hoof bandage around the hoof.

Hoof bandage

This emergency bandage has to see to it that the hoof stays reasonably clean until the vet arrives to put a proper bandage on.

First put sterile gauze, perhaps soaked in antiseptic, on the cleaned wound. The whole hoof (sole, wall, balls) should then be covered up to two centimetres above the coronet with cotton wool. A super alternative for this is a baby's disposable nappy. Then wrap the whole hoof with strong tape. The best way is to prepare a type of sole for the hoof, by sticking 20-25 cm long strips of tape over each other, making a square. This is then stuck on the bottom of the horse's foot (while someone holds the foot). Wrap some tape around the ends and finish by including the coronet of the hoof as well.

Remember to leave approximately 2 cm of the cotton wool above the bandage.

4. Prevention:
Inspect the area where the horse lives on a regular basis. Choose bridlepaths carefully, with the aim of an injury-free ride.

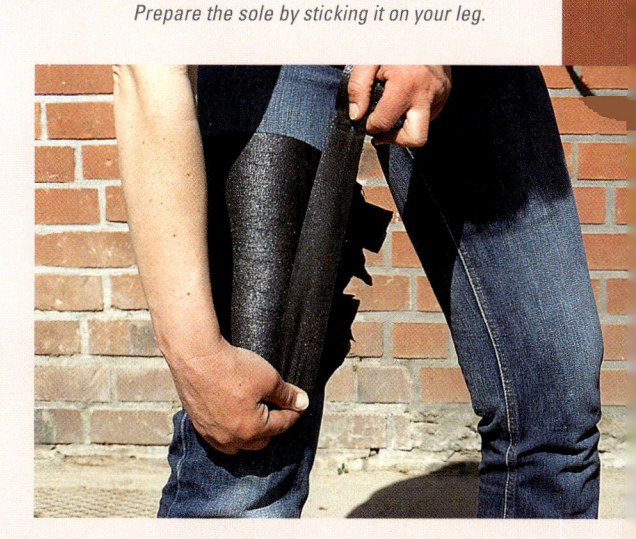

Prepare the sole by sticking it on your leg.

First Aid

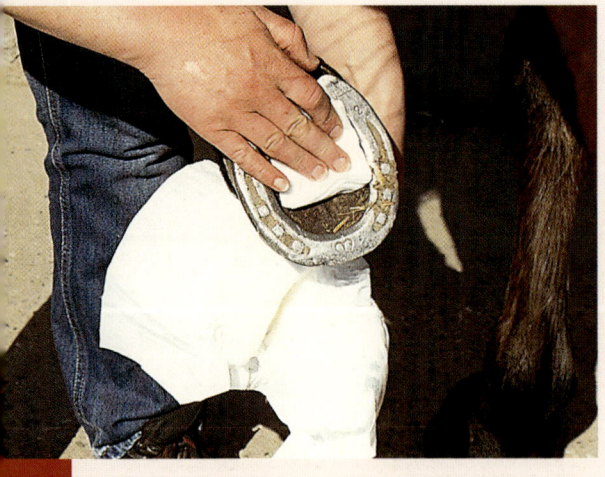

Cover the wound after cleaning with sterile gauze.

Press the prepared sole on the hoof, fold the edges around ...

Disposable nappies are ideal for use as hoof bandages.

... and wrap some tape around the coronet.

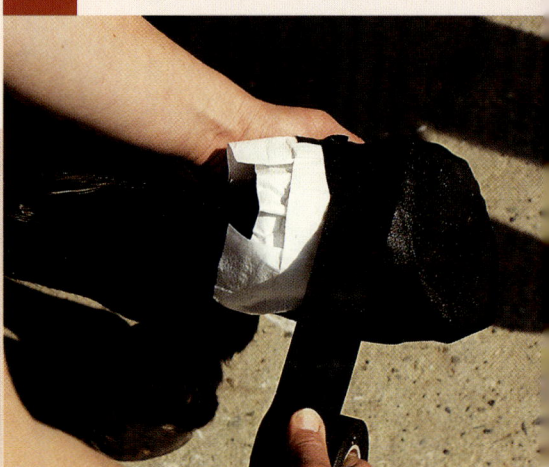

Laminitis

This illness of the horse causes extreme pain in the soles of the feet. The horse will predominantly try not to put any weight on the affected feet. It is seldom that this occurs in only one foot, or in all four at the same time. It is of utmost importance to react swiftly. The sooner the horse can be treated, the better the long-term outcome.

1. Main causes:
There are many theories, not all of which have been explored. Here are four theories:

Nutrition-induced laminitis:
This mainly affects ponies and horses that are "good doers". High proportions of protein-rich feed trigger this response, for exam-

Illnesses

ple fresh young grass in spring and also the sunny days in autumn and winter. Excessive amounts of carbohydrates in composite food can also cause this.

Acute laminitis:
Causes are too many rides across hard surfaces in fast gaits. This is more prominent in horses with thin soles or without shoes.

Toxic laminitis:
This type of laminitis can be induced at birth, mainly when the placenta is retained in the mare.

Drug-related laminitis:
Some types of cortisone can cause laminitis as well.

2. **Symptoms:**
- The horse tends to stand with the front legs stretched forward.
- The hoofs are hot.
- You can feel a pulse in the hoof (see hoof injuries).
- The horse does not enjoy moving.
- The horse is reluctant to lift his feet, as the affected hoof will be under even more strain.
- The horse looks anxious.

3. **First aid:**
- Remove all feed (possibly leave the straw).
- Do not force the horse to move.
- Cool the feet, put them in a bucket or spray them with water.
- Wrap cold and wet towels around the hooves.
- Stand the horse on a soft floor.

4. **Prevention:**
- Take time to get the horse used to grazing.
  (For example, over a period of 14 days: 2 days for 15 minutes, 4 days for 30 minutes, 4 days for 45 minutes, 4 days for 60 minutes.)
- Do not leave horses that are prone to laminitis in the paddock, or only allow them out with a muzzle.
- Only feed composite feed when the horse needs to perform.
- Store composite feed out of reach.
- Avoid hard ground (also for driving horses).
- Protect the hooves (shoes, special shoes etc).
- Make sure the placenta is delivered within two hours of foaling.

It is better to fit a muzzle on the horse to restrict feeding, than to keep the horse in the stable to prevent it from grazing.

First Aid

Standing in the stable for too long can easily lead to "tying-up".

Bad weather should be no reason for not working the horse.

Azoturia

Azoturia is a disorder of the muscles of the hindquarters. This is also called "tying-up", or equine rhabdomyolysis.

1. Main causes:
- Irregular exercise (sudden or abrupt pause in training with severe training following).
- Too much glucose in feed (carrots).
- Bracken and "mare's tail" will cause similar symptoms to azoturia.

2. Symptoms:
- Stiff gait of the hind legs.
- Reluctance to move.
- Hardened muscles on the hindquarters.
- Possible circulation problems, with excessive sweating and shivering.
- Urine may be coloured red.
- Pained expression.

2. First aid:
- Keep the horse warm, either with rugs that are changed when wet, or a solarium when available.
- Allow the horse to rest.
- Remove all composite feed.

3. Prevention:
- Regular, daily work.
- Feed according to performance.

Illnesses

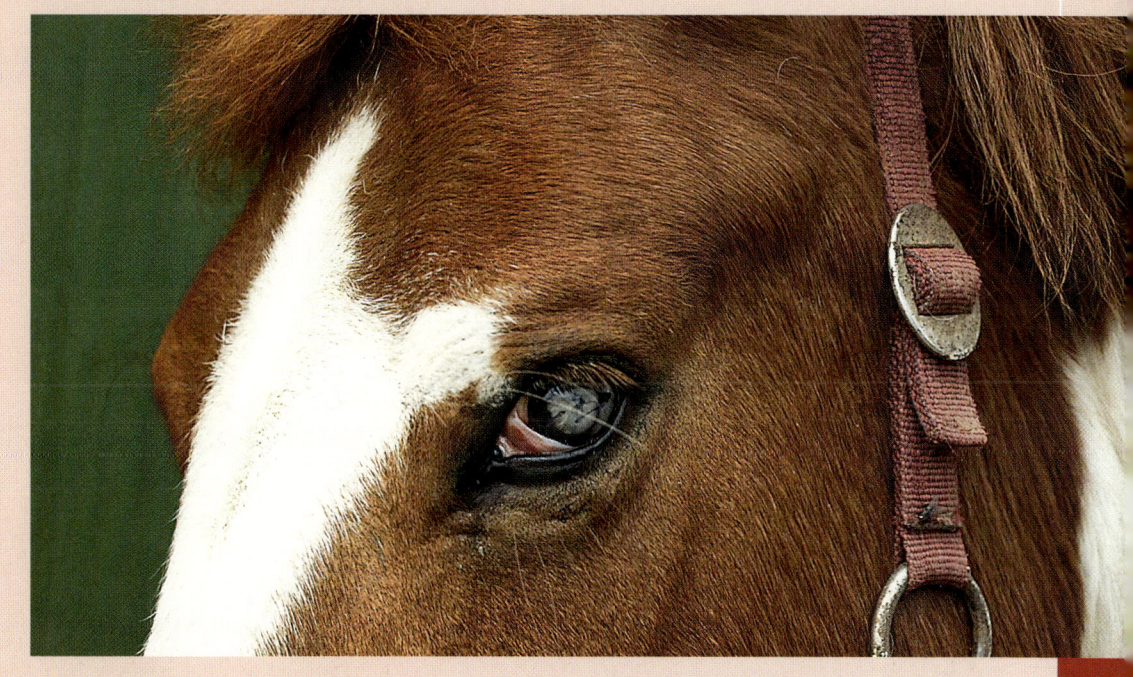

A splinter caused one-sided blindness in this mare as a foal

Eye injuries

These kind of injuries occur mainly in the paddock, when the horse greedily aims to get the best bites.

1. Main causes:
- Twigs.
- Sharp objects.
- Kicks.
- Fly fringes/head collars.

2. Symptoms:
- Visible wounds.
- Swelling around the eyes.
- Tears.
- Discharge of pus.
- Heat.
- Increased rubbing.

3. First aid:
- Try and keep the wound free from insects.
- Prevent rubbing.
- Put the horse in a dark stable.
- Do not attempt to cleanse the wound.

4. Prevention:
- Regular inspection of paddocks.
- Fit fly fringe and head collar properly to avoid them slipping over the eyes.

First Aid

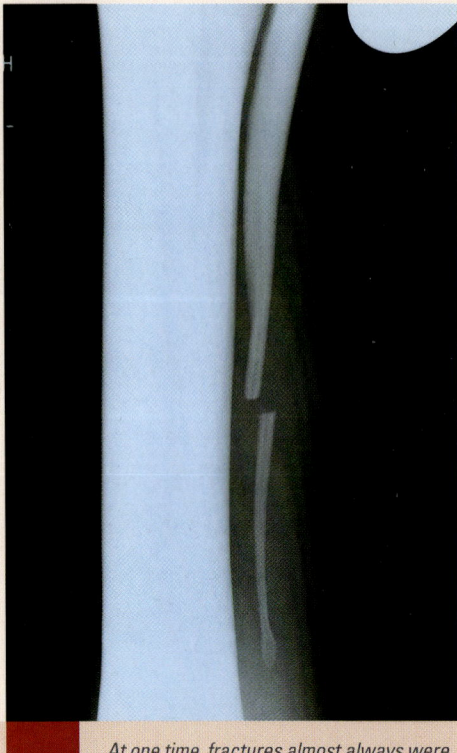

At one time, fractures almost always were a death sentence. Nowadays they can often be mended.

Fractures

This kind of injury is the worst nightmare of every horse owner. However, while at one time fractures would be a death sentence to a horse, this is no longer always the case. Nevertheless, the period of healing is lengthy, very costly and the horse will not necessarily be sound once the bone has recovered.

1. **Main causes:**
   - Kicks.
   - Falls in canter on straight lines or at the trot on the lunge, jumping and when the horse fools around.
   - Traffic accidents.

2. **Symptoms:**
   - The horse is extremely lame.
   - There will be a cracking sound when the leg breaks.
   - With an open wound, the broken bone can be seen through the skin.
   - The leg has a peculiar angle to it.
   - The lower leg swings around helplessly.
   - The affected limbs will swell rapidly.
   - Heat develops.

3. **First aid:**
   - Do not allow the horse to move another centimetre.
   - Call the vet and inform him of your suspicion so the X-ray machine can be brought as well.
   - Cover an open break loosely with a sterile bandage.
   - Calm the horse down.
   - Cover the horse with a sweat sheet.
   - Remove the saddle if it happened while riding.

4. **Prevention:**
Unfortunately even the best care and caution cannot always prevent a fracture.

Shock

When a horse is in shock, this is very serious, as the horse can die! Call the vet urgently.

1. Main causes:
- Loss of blood from an open wound, diarrhoea with high loss of liquid, excessive sweating with insufficient drinking.
- Heart problems.
- Burn wounds.
- High performance at extreme temperatures.
- Eating something poisonous, as well as toxic situations due to illness.
- Spinal injuries.
- Accidents.
- Stress.
- Allergies/nettle-rash (anaphylactic shock).

2. Symptoms:
- Restlessness.
- Sweating. In contrast with normal sweat, this will be cold and can cover the whole body of the horse until it drips from the body.
- High pulse (60-130).
- Rapid breathing.
- Pale mucous membranes (in exceptional cases the membranes can also be red or even blue).
- Anxiety.

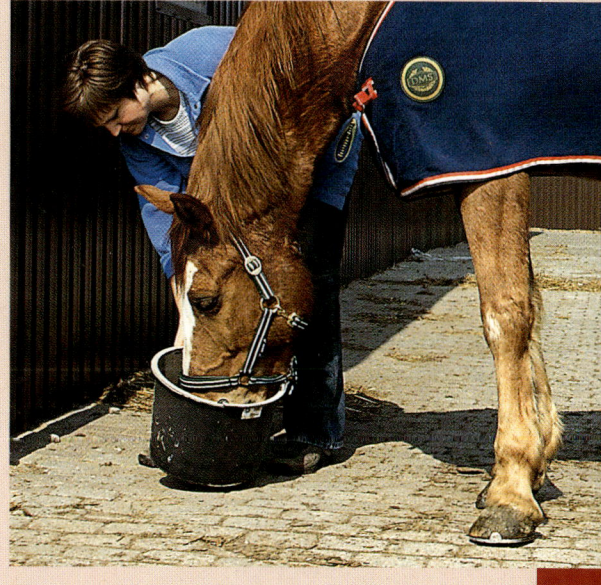

Radiate calmness and offer the warmly covered horse some water.

3. First aid:
- Cover the horse with a rug.
- Offer water to try and balance the loss of liquid.
- Stay calm.
- Avoid cold water when the horse is too hot, as this can lead to even worse symptoms.

4. Prevention:
Always provide enough clean water – especially for horses lower in the hierarchy in big herds. Inspect the water at regular intervals and clean and refill dirty troughs immediately. Exercise the horse according to the weather – do not expect peak performance in extremely hot weather.

Pay attention when the horse has diarrhoea. Call the vet without delay when it is too runny, or after about three days when it has the consistency of a paste.

First Aid

When riding in groups, one person should tend to the horse while someone else goes to fetch help. Be warned: some horses may become even more upset when its friend leaves to call for help. For this reason, it is sometimes better to leave the horse and fetch help on foot.

Every rider should carry a small first aid bag on the saddle. Unfortunately too few riders do. Only when you have bandages available can you apply something to an injury. Otherwise you have to depend on tissues and torn-off sleeves, or something similar.

When the horse is severely injured the vet has to go to the location where the horse was injured. Keep the horse as warm as possible by not removing saddles etc. to prevent shock setting in.

If the horse is still able to walk, dismount and lead it back to the stable or somewhere closer where it can be accommodated in order for you to call for help.

A clean T-shirt can become a makeshift bandage on a hack.

First aid out hacking

An emergency in the stable or in the paddock is quite bad enough. It can be much worse to have an emergency on a hack – especially when one is out alone! The single rider should be responsible enough to take a mobile telephone with them on a hack. A telephone can mean the difference between life and death, for either the horse or the rider.

Always notify someone in the stable when you leave, providing details of the route you intend to take. This way, help can be sent when you do not return within a reasonable time (or when your horse returns without you…).

Never leave the injured horse alone, rather fetch help on foot. A mobile phone would be the easiest solution.